How to Analyze People

The Ultimate Guide to Developing Laser-Sharp People-Reading Skills, Uncovering their True Intentions and Determining their Personality Type

Table of Contents

Introduction

Congratulations on downloading your personal copy of *How to Analyze People*. Thank you for doing so.

The following chapters will discuss some of the many ways you can learn how to tell what people are really thinking.

You will discover how important it is to take into account all their body language cues and how they communicate style.

The final chapter will explore how to understand people's feelings.

There are plenty of books on this subject on the market, thanks again for choosing this one! Every effort was made to ensure it is full of as much useful information as possible. Please enjoy!

Personality Types

The reasoning behind the Myers-Briggs test is to figure out different psychological types and to make them easily understood and useful for people. The theory is that the random variations of people's behavior are very consistent and orderly due to differences in how people use the judgment and perception.

Perception is being aware of ideas, happenings, people, and things. Judgment is the ways of making conclusions on what one perceives. If people are different in how they come to conclusions and what the perceive, then it is reasonable for people to have differences in their skills, motivations, values, reactions, and interests.

When the Myers-Briggs test was developed, they wanted everyone to be able to figure out what group they belonged to.

The main reason to decide to take the MBTI test is to find out what your personality type is. Many studies have been done over the past 40 years. They have proved it to be reliable and valid. When you decide to find your personality type, make sure the test you are using has been validated.

This theory was introduced in the 20s by Carl Jung. The MBTI tool was created in the 40s by Isabel Briggs Myers. The research behind it was done in the 40s and 50s. The research is continuing and provides users with new information about psychological types and how it's used. Millions have taken the Indicator test every year since it was first published in 1962.

Type is more than the four preferences. MBTI is a way of telling people about their interaction with their four mental functions and the ones they like to use first. This is referred to as type dynamics. It's the most important part of figuring out your results.

Here are some facts about some type dynamics:

- The dominant function will influence you most.

- The second strongest is the auxiliary. It helps to support and balance the dominant.

- The third is the tertiary function.

- The fourth function is the least strong. It is usually referred to as the inferior function.

- Every person will show one preference first to the world.

- The eight different functions are expressed differently in the outer and inner world.

- The two middle preferences are referred to as the function pair.

- Within the course of life, different preferences might come out and get used more easily and more than normal. This is called type development.

Here are the sixteen different personality types:

ENTJ

These people will be decisive and frank, and the will assume leadership. They are quick to notice inefficient and illogical policies and procedure. They will develop complicated systems to solve problems. They enjoy setting goals and long-term planning. They are well read and informed. They like to expand their knowledge and give it to others. They can be quite forceful when presenting their ideas.

ENFJ

These people are responsible, responsive, empathetic, and warm. They are very attuned to the motivations, needs, and emotions of other people. They will find potential in everybody. They try to help others reach their potential. They often act as catalysts for groups and individual growth. They are responsive and loyal to criticism and praise. They give leadership to inspire. They like to facilitate others when in a group. They are very sociable.

ESFJ

These people are cooperative, conscientious, and warm-hearted. They like to have harmony around them. They work hard to establish this. They work well with others to get tasks done on time. They are loyal and will follow through on the minutest of details. They can see what others need in their everyday lives and try to give it to them. They like to be appreciated for what they do and who they are.

ESTJ

These people are matter-of-fact, realistic, and practical. They move quickly to make decisions and implement them. They like to organize people and projects to do things. They get results in the best way possible. They focus on details. They have a set of standards. They will follow these systematically. They want others to do the same. They can be forceful when they want to implement their plans.

ENTP

These people are outspoken, alert, stimulating, ingenious, and quick. They get resourceful when faced with challenging problems to solve. They can adapt to making visionary possibilities and analyze them critically. They can read others well. They are generally bored and never do anything the same way twice. They go from one interest to another.

ENFP

These people are imaginative and enthusiastically warm. They look at life as being full of possibilities. They can connect information and events quickly and very confidently by the patterns they see. They need affirmation from others. They easily give support and appreciation. They are flexible and spontaneous and rely on their knowledge of improvisation. They are fluent verbally.

ESFP

These people are accepting, friendly, and outgoing. These people are love material comforts, people, and life. They like working with other people and making things happen. They approach their work realistically and with common sense. They make their work fun. They are spontaneous and flexible. They can adapt to new environments and people easily. They learn by trying new skills with others.

ESTP

These people are tolerant and flexible. They are focused logically and want immediate results. Theoretically, explanations tend to bore them. They energetically act to get the problem solved. They focus on the present. They enjoy every moment they are with others and are spontaneous. They enjoy material style and comforts. They learn by doing.

INTP

These people try to develop explanations for whatever interests them. They are abstract and theoretical. Ideas interest them more than social interactions. They are adaptable, flexible, contained, quiet. They have an ability to focus on solving problems that interest them. They are always analytical, can be critical, and skeptical.

INFP

These people are loyal to people that mean something to them. They are loyal to their values. They are idealistic. They want their lives to be in tune with their values. These people can motivate their ideas. They have the ability to see possibilities. They are very curious. They try to understand others and want to help them reach their potential. They are accepting, flexible, and adaptable unless one of their values gets threatened.

ISFP

These people are kind, sensitive, friendly, and quiet. They live in the moment and with what is happening around them. They want their own space and work in their own time. They are committed to their values. They are loyal to people who mean something to them. They don't like conflicts or disagreements. They won't force their values and opinions on others.

ISTP

These people are flexible and tolerant. They observe quietly unless a problem appears. They will act quickly to find solutions. They evaluate what makes things work. They look at huge amounts of data to figure out the core of simple problems. They value efficiency. They organize facts by using logic. They are interested in cause and effect.

INTJ

They have a wonderful drive for carrying out their ideas and reaching their goals. They have originals minds. They can see patterns quickly. They develop long-range perspectives. When they commit to a job, they will organize and see it through. They are independent and skeptical. They hold high standards to performance and competence for others as well as themselves.

INFJ

These people want material possessions. They look for meaningful relationships. They want to connect to their ideas and seek meaning. They need to know what motivates others. They are committed to their values. They are conscientious. They will develop a vision about the best way to serve the common good. They are decisive and organized when implementing their vision.

ISFJ

These people are conscientious, responsible, friendly, and quiet. They are committed to meet their obligations. They are accurate, painstaking, and thorough. They see certain things about people and remember them if they are important to them. They are considerate, loyal, and concerned with how others feel. They need a harmonious and orderly environment at home and work.

ISTJ

These people are dependable, thorough, serious, and quiet. Their thoroughness earns them success. They are responsible, realistic, matter-of-fact, and practical. They will logically decide what needs to be done and work at it despite distractions. They like to have everything organized and orderly like their life, home, and work. They value loyalty and traditions.

Body Language Cue

Relationships are created by communication. We share with each other. When we share, we can understand better, and this helps our relationships grow.

The tricky aspect is most of our communication isn't verbal. You may not actually use words to tell someone that you are upset with them. You might draw away from them. You might cross your arms, turn your feet to the door and won't make contact. If they don't see your signals, they won't realize that something is off.

Even if they pick up on your body signals, they might not realize what their body is saying. If your body language is standoffish and cold, people might not approach you, even if you desire them to.

You can make body language part of your interactions. From body movements to facial expressions, what we don't say will still give off a lot of information.

Body language accounts for about 60 percent of everyday communication. It is important to understand body language. You also need to pay attentions to context clues. In most cases, you need to look at body signals as a group instead of one action.

Here are some things to look for when interpreting body language.

Facial Expressions

Think about how much you can tell about a person with just their facial expressions. A smile could mean happiness or approval. A frown might signal unhappiness or disapproval. In other cases, facial expressions might reveal the true feeling about a certain situation. You might say that you feel fine, but your face says something totally different.

Here are some emotions that could be revealed by facial expressions:

- Contempt
- Desire
- Excitement
- Confusion
- Fear
- Disgust
- Surprise
- Anger
- Sadness
- Happiness

The look on a person's face can help us figure out if we believe or trust what the other person is saying. The expression that is trusted most is one with a slightly raised eyebrow along with a slight smile. This expression shows both confidence and friendliness.

Facial expressions are the most universal body language forms. The expressions that are used to show happiness, sadness, anger and fear are the same throughout the entire world. Along with the expressions of sadness, surprise, fear, anger, and joy.

We will make judgments about a person's intelligence that is based on the facial expressions. Individuals that had prominent noses and narrower faces are considered to be intelligent. People who have joyful and smiling expressions are thought to be more intelligent than people who look angry.

The Eyes

The eyes are often called the windows to the soul because they can reveal a lot about what someone is thinking or feeling. When you start a conversation with others, notice their eye movements. This is an important and natural part of communicating. Some things you might notice are whether or not they make eye contact, if the pupils are dilated, or if there is too much blinking. When we talk about smiling, the mouth might lie but the eyes won't. True smiles will reach the eyes and crinkle the skin around them. People will sometimes smile to hide what they really are feeling and thinking. The next time you are wondering if somebody's smile is true, look for the crinkles in the corners of the eyes. If you don't see any, their smile is hiding something.

When looking at a person's body language, watch for these signals:

Pupil Size: Light within the environment does control dilation, but emotions can also change the pupil's size. You might have heard the expression bedroom eyes being used to describe how someone looks when they are physically attracted to someone else. Heavily dilated eyes could indicate a person is aroused or interested.

Blinking: This is a natural function. You need to see whether they are blinking too little or too much. People blink more when they feel uncomfortable or distressed. Blinking less indicates they are trying to control their eye movements intentionally. An example would be a poker player might try to blink less because they are trying to seem unexcited about what they were dealt.

Eye Gaze: If a person looks right into your eyes while talking to you, it shows that they are paying attention and interested in what you are talking about. Excessive eye contact might begin to feel threatening. If someone is looking at you, and their look makes you feel uncomfortable, especially if they don't blink, something could be up, and they could be lying. Most people will hold eye contact for only ten seconds a bit longer if we are listening. Looking away a lot and breaking eye contact could indicate the person is trying to hide their feelings. They might be feeling uncomfortable or distracted.

The Mouth

Mouth movements and expressions can also help with reading someone's body language. If someone chews on their lower lip, it might indicate they're feeling insecure, fear, or worry.

If they cover their mouth when they cough or yawn, might mean they are being polite or trying to cover a disapproving frown. Smiling is the best body signal, but smiles might get interpreted in different ways. A person's smile could be genuine, or it could be expressing cynicism, sarcasm, or false happiness.

Look at the lips and mouth when evaluating body language.

Turned down or up: Subtle changes in a person's mouth might be an indicator of what someone is feeling. If their mouth is turned up a bit, could mean they are feeling optimistic or happy. A mouth that is turned down might indicate disapproval, sadness, or an outright grimace.

Covering the mouth: If someone is hiding an emotional reaction, they may cover their mouth to hide smirks or smiles.

Lip biting: People bite their lips if they feel stressed, anxious, or worried.

Pursed lips: Tightening of a person's lip may indicate distrust, disapproval, or distaste.

Gestures

Gestures are the most obvious and direct signals a person can give. Pointing, waving, or using fingers to show numbers are easy to understand and common. Some might be cultural, so giving a peace sign or thumbs-up in a different country may mean totally different things.

Here are some gestures and their meanings:

The "V" sign: This is made by holding up the middle and index fingers separate to make a V-shape. This could mean victory or peace in certain countries. In Australia and the United Kingdom, this symbol could have an offensive meaning if the back of a person's hand is facing outward.

The "okay" gesture: This is made by touching the index finger and thumb to form a circle while holding up the other fingers. In the United States, this means all right or okay. In parts of Europe, this can imply you are nothing. In certain South American countries, this symbol is a vulgar gesture.

A thumbs down or up: This gesture is a sign of disapproval and approval.

A clenched fist: This can show either solidarity or anger in certain situations.

Legs and Arms

The legs and arms are useful when conveying nonverbal information. Crossed arms indicate defensiveness. If a person crosses their legs away from someone else, it can show discomfort or dislike for that person.

Other signals like opening the arms wide might be indicating they are trying to be more commanding and be seen as larger. If a person is keeping their arms close to their body, they might be trying to make themselves seem smaller or trying to draw attention away from them.

Here are some signals that legs and arms might show:

Crossed legs: This might show a person needs privacy or feeling closed off from their surroundings.

Fidgeting or tapping finger rapidly: This could mean that the person is frustrated, impatient, or bored.

Holding hands behind their back: This may show that they are feeling angry, anxious, and bored.

Standing with their hands on their hips: This can show that they are in control or it might be a sign of aggression.

Crossed arms: This may show a person is feeling closed-off, self-protective, or defensive.

Posture

The way we hold ourselves is another part of body language. Posture refers the way we hold our bodies and their physical form. Posture can tell a lot about how someone is feeling and possibly hints about their personality characteristics like if they are submissive, open, or confident.

Sitting straight could indicate that the person is paying attention and focused on what is going on. Sitting hunched forward can say they are indifferent or bored.

Notice these signals about a person's posture and what it is saying:

Closed posture: This is indicative of trying to hide their trunk by hunching forward and crossing their legs and arms. This posture might indicate anxiety, unfriendliness, and hostility.

Open posture: This is where someone is keeping their trunk exposed and open. This is showing willingness, openness, and friendliness.

Copying Body Language

If you've ever met with someone and you realized they were mimicking your moves? This is a good sign. When we feel comfortable with another person, mirroring their body language is something that happens unconsciously. It shows the meeting is going well and they want to understand what you are saying. Knowing this will be helpful when you are negotiating, it shows what the other is thinking about the situation.

Raised Eyebrows

Raised eyebrows signals discomfort. There are three emotions that will cause your eyebrows go up. They are fear, worry, and surprise. Try to raise your eyebrows when you are talking with a friend. You won't be able to. If somebody you are talking to raises theirs, and you aren't talking about anything the is causing fear, worry, or surprise, then something else is happening.

Exaggerated Nodding

Excessive nodding show anxiety about being approved. If you are telling somebody something and they begin nodding excessively, this indicates that they are worried about your impression of them. They might also be wondering if you doubt their ability to follow instructions.

Clenched Jaw

A clenched jaw, furrowed brow, or tightened neck are signs of stress. It doesn't matter what they are saying, these are all signs of discomfort. The conversation could be heading into something they are feeling anxious about. Their mind might be somewhere else. They could be focusing on what is stressing them out. The main thing is to watch for what they are saying and what their body language is telling you.

Personal Space

Has someone ever told you they needed personal space? Have you begun to feel uncomfortable when someone gets too close to you?

The term refers to how close people stand to each other when interacting. Just like facial expressions and body movements can show a lot of nonverbal information, this space between individuals can work as well.

There are four levels of distance that can occur in certain situations:

Intimate Distance: This is about 6 to 18 inches apart. This distance indicates a close relationship and a level of comfort with each other. It usually occurs with contact like touching, whispering, or hugging.

Personal Distance: This is about one and a half to four feet apart. This distance will occur between close friends and family members. The closer they can stand when interacting could show how intimate their relationship is.

Social Distance: This is around 4 to 12 feet. This distance is used to people who are acquaintances. With someone like a co-worker that you see many times during a week, you may feel comfortable being closer to them. If you don't know someone too well, like a delivery driver that you only see once in a while, a distance of about 10 to 12 feet will feel more comfortable.

Public Distance: This is about 12 to 25 feet. This level of distance is seen at public speaking events. Talking to a class of students of giving a presentation are great examples of these.

It is important to note that the distance that people need to feel comfortable varies with each culture. Some examples are seen with the differences with people from North American and Latin cultures. People of Latin decent are comfortable standing closer to each other when they interact. North Americans need a lot of personal space.

Understanding body language will help you be able to communicate better with others as well as interpreting what they are trying to tell you. If you can't read their thoughts, you might learn something from their body language. This is very true when their words and their body is saying two different things.

You need to learn more about how to improve your communication to get better at telling people what we are feeling without speaking one word.

Introvert or Extrovert

Recent studies say that humans are actually more shallow than we once thought. People can tell an extrovert from an introvert just by looking at their faces. As with other characteristics, facial expressions can tell a lot about a person. In the case of extroversion and introversion, people who have certain traits like feminine features, and bright eyes are thought to be more extroverted. Feminine facial features are seen to be more trustworthy and happier. People associate characteristics like friendliness, competence, and dominance with certain facial features.

This is a just a part of a phenomenon called faceism. It has been referred to through history as physiognomy. It has created bad consequences for society. Thanks to this, researchers can argue that the appearance of people's faces can sway how we vote, the people we hire, and the decisions we make in court. Politicians whose face shows competence are usually elected into an official position. Studies have shown that people who live in conservative states see that certain politician's faces look more Republican. This then results in these people getting the most votes.

If a business person looks competent, then they will more than likely get a higher salary.

The same thing also influences military rankings. If a soldier has a more dominant-looking face, they will get chosen for higher ranking positions. As equally problematic is people who have guilty or untrustworthy faces are usually convicted in court. A person with untrustworthy features will have high eyebrows and prominent cheekbones. Individuals that don't have these features have a better chance of getting loans and finding financial investments.

People tend to jump to conclusions about a person's character based on their facial features. This will affect and damage how we interact in society. We like to think that our choices and judgments are consistent, impartial, rational, and based on reliable information. Most of the time they are based on irrelevant and superficial factors. This is a human trait that must be corrected. Faces will never be valid predictors of someone's traits.

Looking at a face is helpful when looking for feelings, gender, or age. We need to question our perceptions. We must guard ourselves against letting our choices be based on superficial clues. In some instances, educating people could help reduce stereotyping. In other instances, more studies are needed to figure out the best way to reduce our influences based on facial appearance.

We need to educate ourselves about political views of certain politicians. This way, we will have fewer assumptions about them based on their facial appearance. People won't get rid of these assumptions, and this will lead to more problems. With the technology we have to genetically design a child with certain traits, we have to avoid scenarios where people want to create children that fit into certain criteria.

It is important to realize that we can't rely on our assumptions of someone as an indication of their character or personality. We have to challenge these assumptions by getting to know about them before we increase their salary, vote for them, or choose to hire them. By reflecting on our shallow human nature, we could avoid consequences by not judging.

Let's go a bit deeper into telling the difference between extrovert and introvert. The main thing to know is extroversion and introversion and just a spectrum. Many of us fall into this continuum. This means that no one is one way or the other. To quote Carl G. Jung, "There is no such thing as a pure introvert or extrovert. Such a person would be in the lunatic asylum."

To differentiate and introvert from an extrovert, the main difference is how they recharge.

- Extroverts recharge by putting themselves into social situations. They like being in the spotlight and the center of attention. Being alone will totally drain them mentally.

- Introverts will recharge by finding time to be alone. After being in a situation where it's crowded, they need to take a break to get their energy back.

- The last personality is ambivert. This consists of the majority of the population. Ambiverts regain and recharge their energy with a mixture of being alone and socializing.

If this is too vague, let's go a bit deeper.

Extroverts: these people talk the most:

1. Meeting new people won't upset them.

2. They like for others to pay attention to them.

3. They can talk to anyone about anything.

4. The will initiate and engage conversations.

5. Social situations and people energize and excite them.

Introverts: these people think more than speak:

1. They don't like meeting new people.

2. They don't like being in the spotlight.

3. They don't like to chit chat.

4. They use their ears and eyes instead of their mouths.

5. They recharge by being alone.

Ambiverts: These people are a mix of the two:

1. They don't mind talking to new people, but they like it better if it is friends.

2. They don't mind attention, but more often they stand to the side.

3. They will sometimes find small talk insincere.

4. They like to be quiet in a conversation but will share if they are passionate about something.

5. They sometimes wonder if they need some external stimulation or some time alone.

Some researchers think our tendencies could be related to genes. They have discovered that introverts and extroverts get aroused differently. This means that each one takes different states of stimulation to excite them.

People that are extroverts aren't easily excited. This means they will look for what excites and stimulates them in their surroundings or other external means. Introverts are just the opposite.

Why does this matter to me? You may have taken several personality tests and know some things. For the majority, we don't know who our true selves are.

Extroverts are usually told to quit being obnoxious. Introverts are looked at as anti-social. Ambiverts are thought to have split personalities. The truth is you need to learn who you are. This will allow you to know yourself better.

You might learn something about other types, and how to interact with others, this will improve your romantic and social lives.

Every one of us is unique. We must learn to embrace this. There isn't a preferred personality. We need to accept people for who they are.

Introverts like to socialize a little at a time. They will retreat if they need to. These people are thought to be shy and lack communication skills. Don't try to be more extroverted. When you are thinking deeply and expressing your thoughts, you are making meaningful and authentic relationships.

Try not to criticize extroverts for their annoying or obnoxious traits. They are only expressing their emotions. They could be consistently reaching out to you. You need to protect the time you have alone, so you don't strain your mental state.

Extroverts don't think there is anything wrong with speaking up. Others think that you hog the limelight since you feel insecure. Don't let that stop you from sharing your opinions and thoughts.

You like to encourage others but remember that introverts need their own space. Find the correct time to comfort others or your empathy might backfire.

Ambiverts are not abnormal. Have you ever been confused with whether or not you are an introvert or extrovert? The majority of the human race are ambiverts. They have traits from each side of the spectrum. You are more flexible since you are comfortable being with people and being alone.

You are more stable emotionally. You find balance with being sensitive but aren't influenced easily. The stability makes you intuitive. You know when to shut up and when to speak.

It really doesn't matter where you stand in the continuum. You are special. You need to embrace your true self.

Communication Style

If we are going to develop assertive and effective communication skills, we have to be able to identify the different communication styles and know which ones we use more often. How can you tell the difference and is there a place and time for each in different situations?

Communicating assertively means you respect others and yourself. It means you can express your feelings and thoughts clearly with direct, honest, and open communication.

Being more assertive doesn't mean that you will get what you want. It could get you a compromise. If you don't get what you want, you will know that you handled the situation the best you could and there aren't any bad feelings between you and the other people involved.

Communicating assertively isn't a skill that is reserved for just a few, anybody can do it. It will take practice and time if you aren't used to communicating this way. This is a technique that you can master in the comfort of your own home, on your own time. You can do it with a friend or by yourself. Think about how the person you will be talking to might react and how you will cope with the situation.

Before you decide that you want to communicate assertively, you need to understand what your normal communication style is. There are five different styles. Many people use different styles with different situations. Most fall automatically into one style; this is what is referred to as a default style.

The five communication styles are:

- Manipulative
- Submissive
- Passive-aggressive
- Aggressive
- Assertive

Each style has its own language and behaviors.

Manipulative

This communication style is shrewd, calculating, and scheming. These communicators are skilled at controlling or influencing other for their own good. The words they speak will always have an underlying message that the other person will not be aware of.

Behavioral Characteristics:

- Uses fake tears
- Makes others feel sorry for them or obliged.
- Indirectly asks for their needs to be met.
- Controls other in a sneaky way such as by sulking.
- Cunning

Nonverbal Behavior:

- Facial expressions
- Voice might be high pitched, ingratiating, envious, or patronizing.

People who are on the receiving end of their behavior might feel:

- Resentful

- Annoyed

- Irritated

- Angry

- Frustrated

- Guilty

- Others feel confused as to where they stand with a manipulative person and get annoyed with working so hard figuring out what is happening.

You might hear something like this from manipulative people, "I can't believe you bought those expensive chocolates. I would love to be able to afford those chocolates." Or something similar to this, "With everything else I had to do, I didn't have time to shop for a new dress. I hope this one doesn't look too out of style on me." This person is fishing for compliments.

Submissive

This communication style likes to please others. They don't like conflict. This person acts like everybody else's needs are more important than theirs. They think that other people can contribute more and have more rights.

Behavioral Characteristics:

- Won't express desires or feelings.

- Won't take compliments.

- They blame others for things that happen.

- They feel like the victim.
- They opt out of activities.
- They yield to other's preferences.
- They discount their needs and rights.
- They won't make decisions or responsibility.
- They will avoid all confrontations.
- They always apologize.
- They won't ask for what they want.

Nonverbal Behavior:
- Soft voice
- Small posture – try to make themselves invisible
- Gestures – fidget and twist
- Facial expressions – won't make eye contact
- Spatial position – they make themselves small
- Submissive behavior – marked with a victim's attitude. They have a victim's mentality. They will refuse to try new things that could help them.

People who receive their behavior will feel:
- You can be taken advantage of.
- They can discount you since you never know what you want.
- Guilty
- Frustrated
- Exasperated

- Resent your low energy.

- Stop trying to help you since you reject their efforts.

You might hear this from a submissive person: "I don't know, you pick." "Go ahead and take it. I don't use it anymore." "Nothing's wrong. I'm fine."

Passive-Aggressive Style

This communication style people will seem passive but are pushing their anger so they can deal with their lack of power in indirect ways. POWs will act this way because they are dealing with a huge loss of power. People that act this way feel resentful and powerless. They express these feelings by undermining what they resent even if they undermine themselves. People who exhibit this type of behavior will hurt themselves while trying to hurt others.

Behavioral Characteristics:

- Two-faced – They will be nice to your face but talk bad about you when you aren't around. They will tell rumors or try to sabotage them. They will try to hurt another person by making their food too spicy or sabotaging their equipment to cause failure.

- Gossip

- Patronizing

- Sulky

- Complaining

- Unreliable

- Devious

- Sarcastic

- Indirectly aggressive

Nonverbal Behavior:

- Spatial position – They stand too close or touches to pretend to be friendly and warm.

- Facial expression – They will usually look innocent and sweet.

- Gestures – will be quick and jerky.

- Posture – is usually asymmetrical. They will stand with their hand on a hip with their hip forward.

- Voice – They speak with a super sweet voice.

People who receive their behavior will feel:

- Resentful

- Hurt

- Angry

- Confused

A passive-aggressive person might say things like, "Do it your way, my ideas wasn't any good." They might put a bit of a bite of irony or sarcasm like, "You always know what to do." They might even say things like, "Don't worry about me, I can do this by myself like always."

Aggressive

These people are all about winning and usually at somebody else's expense. These people will behave like their needs are all that matters. Their rights are all that matter, and they contribute more than others. This communication style is ineffective because the message content might get lost since others will be too busy reacting to its delivery.

Behavioral Characteristics

- Bullying
- Intimidating
- Unpredictable, explosive
- Belligerent
- Abrasive, demanding
- Out to win
- Achieving goals at the expense of others
- Hostile
- Loud
- Threatening
- Frightening

Nonverbal Behavior

- Spatial position – They like to stand over other people. They will invade your personal space.
- Facial expression – They will look like they are glaring, frowning, and scowling.
- Gestures – Their gestures will be jerky and sharp, fast, and big.
- Posture – They try to look bigger than the others.
- Voice – They are extremely loud.

People who receive their behavior will feel:

- Problems and mistakes won't get reported to the aggressive person because they might blow up. Other people are scared of being humiliated, exploited, or railroaded.

- Others will lose respect for the aggressive person.

- Afraid

- Hurt

- Degraded

- Humiliated

- Vengeful

- Resentful

- Uncooperative

- Aggressive

- Defensive

- Fight back

You might hear things from an aggressive person like, "You are insane!" "Do it this way!" "You did it wrong!" They might also start being insulting, blaming, threatening, calling names, and sarcasm.

Assertive

This type of behavior is from people who have high self-esteem. This is the most effective and healthiest style of communicating. This is the sweet spot between seeming too passive and too aggressive. People who are assertive have the confidence to communicate without manipulating or playing games.

These people know their limits and won't let themselves be pushed just because somebody needs or wants something. It is surprising that assertive gets used the least.

Behavior Characteristics

- Accepts compliments

- Asks for their needs to be met directly.

- Accepts they might be rejected.

- Makes their own choices and takes responsibility.

- Emotionally and socially expressive.

- Respectful of other people's rights and protective of their own.

- Achieve their goals without hurting others.

Nonverbal Behavior

- Spatial position – They are respectful of others and in control.

- Facial expression – They make eye contact

- Gestures – Expansive, rounded, and even

- Posture – They don't fidget. They are relaxed. They will stand tall. They will be symmetrically balanced. They will keep an open posture.

- Voice – Their voice will have a medium pitch with volume and speed.

People who receive their behavior might feel:

- Respect

- They can take care of themselves.

- They can accept compliments and justified criticism.

- They know their position with this person.

- They can rely on their word.

An assertive person will say things like, "I can't help you move because I have to volunteer at the senior center, I'm sorry." "Could you please lower the volume? I am trying to concentrate on writing."

Understanding the Different Styles

Having an understanding of these styles of communication will help you know how to effectively react if you are confronted with a person who is being difficult. It will help you see that you aren't being assertive or behaving right. You are the only one who can choose what communication style to use. Assertive is always the best. Different styles are necessary for certain situations. You will need to be submissive if you are faced with an attack like a hijacking or mugging.

You need to have a high level of self-awareness to have good communication skills. When you are able to understand your communication style, it will be easier to see any areas that need improving.

If you really want to strengthen your relationships, decrease anxiety, and reduce stress due to conflict, you must practice assertiveness. This will help to build better relationships professionally and personally, reduce guilt, and diffuse anger.

The main rule to effective communication is: To have good communication you need to be a responsible communicator.

Avoiding False Assumptions

Everybody makes assumptions. It happens all the time. Assumptions can be about anything or anyone.

We all like to think we know what others are thinking. We love to this we know why someone did something. We really don't know so we just guess due to wishful thinking, past experiences, or our imagination.

We also like to think we know why a certain event took place. We never base this on evidence or fact, we just make a decision and think that it is a fact.

The problem with assumptions is we all do it, and we are usually wrong. We think someone has a certain motivation behind their actions or something happened for a certain reason. We begin to think the assumptions are the truth.

We can do a lot of damage when we confuse assumptions with the truth. A person's significant other could assume they have been cheating on them and accuse them with such conviction that they destroy their love. A CEO of a company might think a loyal employee is giving away secrets to a rival company and accuse them of such. This can cause the employee to lose faith in the company and leave.

We assume all kinds of things every day. Some could be devastating other just trivial little things. Every assumption is faulty.

Why do we put ourselves through this? It is just a part of our nature to base what we think on the world and others, not just facts that we observe but to the extent of what is happening to us on the inside, psychologically.

We like to make judgments based on wishes, expectations, beliefs, and emotions. We don't base our knowledge on events and people we observe in the world.

We confuse these mechanisms with reality. Our assumptions come from these based on our version of reality even if it isn't real.

We don't see how our inner selves are coloring how we understand the world, and things get distorted. If making assumptions starts to become a habit, we become less grounded in reality and more prone to make problems for others and ourselves.

How can we stop making assumptions and begin to base how we see the world and people on facts? Just pause as we begin to assume and just ask, "Is this true?"

If you answered that question with anything other than, "I know this by observing and saw the truth," then we risk making another assumption.

We need to check the facts before we decide on something, we can stop making accusations and prevent difficulties for others and ourselves.

Here are five assumptions we need to stay away from:

People Know What You Want

Not all people are mind readers. We don't know what you want from us unless you tell us.

A lot of people assume we know what they want. They don't take the time to establish a vision or set expectation since they think we know.

Some people over communicate. They will cause confusion by giving too much information that we aren't able to know what is and isn't important.

This assumption can be avoided by doing two things:

First, know that everyone understands what you want. Ask them questions or observe them to make sure they understand.

Second, make them tell you that they understand and will do what you expect.

People Need Incentives

Incentives can cause all kinds of problems.

There is a lot of research that backs this up. These studies say that incentives will cause things to get worse instead of better.

And still, we all continue to assume that everyone wants something in return. This comes from thinking that everyone needs motivation.

Most people are motivated naturally. Demotivation is the actual problem. We need to focus our energy on keeping demotivation from happening.

People Care

This is the total opposite of the above. Not everyone is completed committed.

Many people don't consider what they make their career. Some think of it as just a way to get their bills paid while they are looking for something better.

Most folks are very motivated. They don't leap over buildings or move mountains to make others happy. They only do what they have to.

We need take care not to assume everyone cares. If we want people to care, we have to make it easy for them to care.

People Need Training

Everyone has pet peeves. Someone's pet peeve might be training. Training is sometimes thought to be the solutions to every problem.

We assume that training is all that is needed. They assume that training is going to fix everybody.

Some people love training. Some people have trained for years. Some even volunteer in their spare time.

Training only fixes a small portion of the problem. Training is only responsible for about one percent of helping people.

People Are Content

Just because people don't complain doesn't mean they don't have problems.

Many people are surprised when someone close to them suddenly stops coming around. We just assumed these people were happy since they never complained about anything.

Some people might call them to find out what happened. This doesn't really help anything at all.

A better way would be to just sit and talk to them. Sit down and have an actual conversation with these people. Learn about what they want out of life. What their ambitions are. You could use this information to keep them near you longer.

How to Avoid Making Assumptions

Try to stay open minded and understand where they are coming from. You won't know what others are thinking unless you are psychic.

Start a conversation if something doesn't feel right. Don't try to understand it by yourself. You can't find the right answer if you don't ask.

Don't begin in a place of assumption. Begin with an open heart and mind and find out about them by talking to them.

Many workplaces have problems with communication due to people's habits of assuming too much.

Misinformation

Are you the oldest child and the high achiever? The insecure but peacemaking middle child? The outgoing but spoiled rotten baby?

This question is tricky. Some studies suggest that our ideas about the birth order influence on a person's personality can be wrong, if not total bunk.

A study done by German researchers found personality type was not developed by the family role. Birth order doesn't have any effect on subdimension of openness, imagination, conscientiousness, agreeableness, emotional stability, or extroversion.

The theory that birth order impacts personality goes back to Freud. Alfred Adler, a colleague of his, codified the idea that birth order determines the personality in the 1920s. The oldest child is supposedly anxious, high self-esteem, competitive, high achieving, fearful, jealous, responsible, organized, conservative, exacting, rule-conscious, goal-oriented, directive, conscientious, and serious. The middle child was the people pleasers and mediators who just go with the flow. Pampers babies were the entertainers of the bunch.

The birth order is a great way to break down things. Many feel a connection with the fact that their place in the family helped to determine who they are. It is a great ice breaker at cocktail parties. Some like to share their insight on how their sense of humor was developed because they were the baby and had to get their mother's attention.

Family dynamics and how they parent each child has a huge impact on their children's prescriptive even if the birth order doesn't. Normally, the firstborn will get all the attention with other children getting fussed over less. Many traditional families still treat their female and male children differently. Parents change with time, too. Most of the time the mother might not leave her job until her second baby is born. In this case, this child will get the most attention. Then the fathers who have two families and aren't involved with their first round of children and they have resolved to be a better father to their second family with their younger wife.

The types of families are always changing, and this makes it difficult to make predictions on how children will turn out based on certain factors.

There could be some basis for the differences in birth order personalities with evolutionary biology. The fact that older children do have an advantage when it comes to the competition for attention. There is no competition. The oldest child that takes charges and is assertive could milk the advantage they hold for as long as they can. If they aren't assertive, this might not be the case. Temperament will trump any parenting style, or birth order could bring. We could also assume that a bigger and older child might tend to be a bully toward their siblings, but this will only hold true if that propensity is there in the beginning.

If you bring up the topic of personality and birth order, everybody has an opinion that is either drawn from their grandparents, their families, or their experiences. The science part has always been wobbly. Many people don't find the stereotype to be true to them.

Many theories vary when it comes to personality. There are over a dozen theories on personality by many great psychologists. Everyone is different from each other in many different ways. We still talk about developing personality. We brand personalities as good or successful and conduct tests to see if a person is right for a certain job.

Most definitions of personality will mention several combinations of qualities, traits, and characteristics that will form a person's nature, behavior, and character. These definitions are from assumptions that these traits are fixable. These assumptions turn out to be wrong since each person is different and unique. Let's explore some myths about personality.

Personality is Developed

This so-called development only happens with the process of resultant learning and training. With both nurture and nature, the person's personality is developed during childhood. It is by the process of learning, and unlearning behavioral modification is developed in later years. Being able to sustain this learning and unlearning is highly unlikely. The lack of sustainability is what causes us to fail at helping someone with alcoholism or making poets at will. Branding these behavior modifications as developing personality will help people in business, even though it lacks genuine orientation.

There Are Unsuccessful and Successful Personalities

No one is truly a failure or success. Many successes are because of situations and opportunities. An army commander who is successful in battle happens because of many different factors like time, weather, weaponry, and the men's morale. This doesn't mean that because he is a successful army manager, he will be a successful corporate manager. Branding personalities as unsuccessful, successful, bad or good are very unrealistic.

Leadership is a Personality Trait

Just because someone is successful in a certain situation doesn't mean they will be successful in all situations. We like to think that leadership only exists in certain events. Leadership can be in situations where no leadership is even exhibited. A leader might lead by avoiding any action. People who are just used to exhibit leadership mistake these exhibitions as personality traits.

Personalities Are Typified

Every person has a unique personality. In this sense, personalities can't be termed as types. There are a lot of psychometric and psychological tests that will divide a person under a certain personality type. It might serve many broad purposes. It could hurt the self-image or self-esteem of others.

Human development happens in the minds of people. Every person is unique. Within some parameters of the environment, nurture, and nature, the human mind is constantly adapting to life's situations. Helping the human mind during this adaptation in a complimentary way could result in mutually supportive and universal peace. The trend is to form personality types that suit certain perceptions of living, whether it is administrative, managerial, ideological, theological. The result of all this is contaminating the minds of people who are vulnerable. They get transformed into dictator, terrorists, fundamentalists, militants, and extremists. Nations could prevent people's minds from getting contaminated by individuals who have defective perceptions at little cost as compared to the expenditure on intelligence gathering, weaponry, and armies. In the social order when we look for successful and good types, people who wield power and authority won't view this as helping people do, feel, and think in supportive ways since this might not meet their goals.

Spotting Discrepancies

Almost everybody you know will lie. Some will lie about things that could change their lives and relationships forever.

Most officers within the police force or FBI are able to look at a person's facial expression and body language as signals that someone is lying.

There are several facial expressions that are associated with lying. Some might be caused by physical reactions, chemical reactions, and nervousness.

You need to know how the person normally acts before you proceed.

You need to watch someone while talking to notice what their natural reactions are and this includes tactics they might have. If they exhibit any lying indicators if you ask them more suggestive questions, you can be assured that they are lying.

Here are some indicators to look out for:

Pause of Delay

You ask a friend a question, and they don't respond. After they have thought about it for a minute, they start responding. How long does this delay need to be before you can consider it as an indicator? It depends.

Ask a friend a question like, "On the fifth of July five years ago, what did you do?" They will probably pause before they answer you since it isn't a question that would evoke an immediate response. They are going to have to think about it and even then, won't be able to give a response. Give the question a bit more depth,

"On the fifth of July five years ago, did you kill a man?" If they pause here, you need to get new friends. They will probably give an immediate response of "No!" This is a simple exercise but shows that the delay must be considered within the context of the question.

Nonverbal or Verbal Disconnect

Our brains are wired so that our nonverbal and verbal behaviors will match up. If there is a disconnect, we have to consider it as a deceptive indicator.

A common disconnect to watch for is when someone nods affirmatively while saying the word no or the opposite turning their head side to side and saying yes. If you tried making this response to a question, you would have to force yourself to make the motions. A deceptive person can do it without thinking.

This indicator only works with narrative responses not in short-phrase or one-word responses. If a person's head makes a sharp nodding motion and they say no, this isn't a disconnect it is emphasis. Know that is some cultures nodding doesn't mean yes and a side to side motion won't mean no.

Hiding Their Eyes or Mouth

A person that is deceptive will try to hide their eyes or mouths when lying. There is a natural response to cover a lie, so if their hand goes to their mouth when responding to a question, that's a clue. There is also a response to the person being lied to. If they hide their eyes when responding, they might be indicating that they can't bear to see your reaction to their lie they are telling. This might be done with a hand, or they could close their eyes. We are talking about blinking, but if they close their eyes when responding, this is a deceptive indicator.

Swallowing or Throat-clearing

If someone swallows hard or clears their throat a lot while answering a question, this is a problem. If they continue after they have answered, then that is fine. If they do it just before they answer, several things could be happening. They might be dressing up a lie before they present it to us. The question may have created an anxiety spike that could have caused dryness or discomfort of the throat and mouth.

Hand to Face Activity

Watch out for what a person is doing with their head or face when responding to a question. This could be licking or biting their lips or pulling on their ears or lips. This goes back to high school science. When you asked the question, the question caused a spike in anxiety since a truthful response will incriminate them. It then triggers the nervous system to start working to get rid of the anxiety, and thus drains the blood away from the ears, face, or the extremities. This can cause them to become itchy or cold. Without them realizing it, their hands automatically go to these areas. There could also be rubbing or wringing of their hands. You have just seen another deceptive indicator.

Grooming Gestures

One other way some people could dissipate anxiety is by physical activity by grooming themselves or their surroundings.

A deceptive man may adjust their glasses, cuff, or tie. A woman could straighten her skirt, or move her hair. People sweat it shouldn't bother us. But if they take out a handkerchief to wipe their sweat off their brow this is significant. Straightening up their surrounding is another grooming gesture. After you ask them a question, they suddenly have to move the phone, the knick knacks on the shelf are crooked, or the pencil is out of the box.

Their Voice or Demeanor Changes

If you know how this person talks and their mannerisms, and you ask them a question and their whole demeanor changes, then something is up. If their manners shift radically like going from calm to hyper or mellow to lively, they probably are telling you the truth.

They Won't Say I

If people are lying about themselves, they won't use the words I or me. They will speak of themselves in the third person like, "This girl loves to listen to music." They might even truncate the way they talk like, "Really love to ski." They will do anything to put distance between them and the lie.

They Have an Answer for Everything

Ask anybody what they did last week and they will need to think about it. This is very true of teenagers. They normally can't come up with a good enough story in a hurry. If you ask a young person a question and they have a quick response, then they have rehearsed their response.

They Fuss and Fidget

If a person continues to perform a random activity that isn't necessary like cleaning their glasses, straightening their clothes, cleaning the table, they could be lying. The anxiety and guilt make them restless. This is very true if they are lying to someone they love. If they are lying to a cop, they won't fidget. If they are deceiving their significant other, they can't be still.

They Proclaim Their Honesty

They will try to sell us on the honesty of their answers. They will use phrases to validate their statements like "to be honest." These tip-offs usually invoke religion. For example, I don't know how many times I have heard the phrase "as God as my witness" or "I swear on my grandmother's grave." Truthful people won't go that far.

To sum it up, people who are lying work real hard to sound truthful. They will smile at the correct moment and say what you want to hear. The result will seem fake and contrived. If it feels like you are being taken for a ride, then you probably are. A big toothy smile is representative of a shark. Beware of the sharks.

Understanding Feelings

Would you like to know people better? If so, you have to understand emotions. The beginning point is to look at a big lie we tell ourselves and others.

A very misleading exchange will happen thousands of times every day. An acquaintance is walking toward you. You meet and smile. They say hello and ask you how your day is going. You reply with a generic great and thank them. Communication has happened, or has it?

Within this exchange, there isn't any real information given, and mutual deception has happened. When we asked the question, we are pretending that we have heard and seen the other person. When we answered, we are only following convention but hidden a lot. Why do we do this? Safety. This is normal. That means it is comfortable. Speed. The interaction was fast; this means we don't have to get caught up in any drama. Script. We know what we need to say on the surface.

So? Are we just going to follow the social norm or would it be better to just ignore the other person? The problem with the type of non-communication is what looks like an inquiry. We just walk away from the discussion thinking we know what is happening. We block any real data that might have been there. This type of transaction is the norm for our culture. We have found a way to now have any substantial dialogue. Normal by definition is what feels comfortable. It is what is proper. So, we have become a quick exchange that leads to invaluable data. This is the main reason we can't understand others.

Don't get caught up in this trap. Here is a secret. There will always be more to the story. If you want to understand people better, you will have to dig. You need to actually ask them how they are, and take the time to understand their emotions.

If the topic you want to discuss is challenging and complex, you are going to need more space and time to get a real answer. If a person is going to get vulnerable and reveal things about themselves that are serious, painful, scary, ugly or complicated, they aren't going to do it in public, hurried, and casual setting. If the person knows you don't have time to listen to them, then they aren't going to talk. If you want them to be honest, you have to get real. Let's talk about the three S's:

Safety: Begin by having a trusting relationship. Ask appropriate questions and build trust. Each day ask a question that is a bit more serious than the one you asked yesterday. Be sure there is enough privacy for the serious questions. Take them for a walk, sit next to them, make time and space for them.

Speed: Serious conversations are going to take longer. Set aside no less than one hour if the conversation is a serious one. If you are in a hurry, they are going to be able to tell, and they won't talk.

Script: The way you respond to them will tell them what will happen next. If they can tell you are going by a script, you are sending them a message that this is fake. If you validate their feelings and ideas at the beginning, they will know they can lie. If you try to pull or push them, they are going to know that this isn't a true friendship meeting. If you can take turns with reflecting, recognizing, listening, asking, and sharing as the dialogue goes back and forth. It will also go beyond the surface.

Do you really understand the emotions and feelings of other people? Can you appreciate where they come from with what they are saying or doing?

If we can't feel the emotions they feel, then how can we get in touch with their feelings? We will have no empathy since we don't have a clue about what is happening to them.

We have to be able to get in touch with what they are feeling.

A method that might now work too well is to pay attention to body language. There are some additional tricks you can use.

When you try this, you will quickly feel more compassion and understand what they are feeling.

Clone Their Posture

To understand exactly what is happening to another, you have to grasp onto their emotions while listening to them talk.

Their emotions and feelings can be felt and detected with realism. Hold yourself in the same way they are holding themselves.

- Lean the same way they are.

- Keep your shoulder in line.

- Mimic their facial expressions.

You need to clone their posture and their mannerisms. By doing this, you will be able to experience their frame of mind, temper, and mood.

You will be able to feel this, and you be able to know where they are coming from better.

Pay attention to facial expressions. Mimic it. You will feel different, and very possibly in line with their feelings.

Shoulders will hold onto stress. See how they are positioning their shoulders and mimic it. If they hunch, you hunch. Lean left or right just like they are. This will reproduce their stress level in you.

This works since it puts us in the same state they are in. This is all due to different stimulus in the environment. Instead of have the stimuli affect us, we are placing our minds and body into the same mold, and this makes us feel the exact same things.

Physical Communication

You can learn more from a person by observing how they are holding themselves. If they turn away from you, they might want to flee.

Their hands tell a story, too: Their thoughts can be communicated by their hands. If they are feeling angry, their hands could be clenched in a fist. Holding or cupping their hands could indicate they might be confused.

If they feel relaxed, they might hold their hands to their sides. Having their hands in their pockets is meaningless. Most people do it because it's comfortable.

It's great when someone actually understands what we are saying. With social interactions, we don't know much about each other. We can't see their innermost feelings they might have. Effective communication means we have to understand any feelings that go beyond what is being said.

When we are talking to someone, we know what they are saying and can tell if their words are being carefully selected to hold back their feelings and emotions.

Good communication means we have to understand what they are saying and grasping their feelings as well.

Copying their posture allows us to do that.

Insights to Understand Others

Developing the skill to understand others and empathy is important for your personal relationships. Doctors that listen to the patients won't get sued as often.

You can pretend to understand other's feelings and concerns. Humans are programmed to dislike and detect insincerity.

Pretending to be sincere will be detected by people around you but hints your body is giving off or by a response to a certain question.

Others may not even be aware they are detecting it. They might just feel uncomfortable with what you are talking about, and they feel they can't trust you.

Having false empathy is counter-productive.

If you try to manipulate emotions, they can backfire and won't be worthwhile. People who are truly empathetic get different responses.

Empathy Avoidance and Overload

There are some aspects of being interested in other's concerns and understanding others need to be explored further.

Empathy avoidance is a lack of empathy. This is also called emotional tone deafness.

Empathy avoidance is not likely to be healthy for long-term relationships. If you can shut off some of your responses can help in certain situations. For example:

At Home: Children need vaccinations. In the first few months of their lives, they will have many vaccinations, sometimes more than one at a time. Getting a needle stuck into your leg hurts and they are going to scream.

Parents need to stop their immediate response and know the benefits of them getting their vaccinations. It will help them avoid serious diseases. Don't focus on their distress that will go away shortly.

At Work: Managers need to be able to make good decisions. They can't do this if they are struggling with their stress around them.

They need to be aware of the feelings of others. They need to balance that with logic and reason but not letting themselves become overwhelmed.

In Healthcare: A surgeon that performs emergency surgeries on people who have been in a bad accident needs to use their skills to repair damage in order to save a person's life. They can't take the time to think about how the patient is going to feel later.

When the operation is over, they will need to explain what they did to save this person's life so the patient can come to terms with what happened to them. They have to stay aware that their patient is a real person who has concerns and feelings and will respond accordingly.

Empathy overload can happen if people are exposed to distressing and difficult information.

In these situations, people might find they can't handle their own emotional response to a situation. This might happen if you find out that a close friend is very ill. You want to support and help them, but your feelings are overriding theirs, and you are unable to help them. It can also bother people who work as a social worker, nurse, or medicine.

You need to manage empathy overload by working on self-regulation and self-control. You can manage your emotions and respond to others better.

Conclusion

Thank for making it through to the end of *How to Analyze People*. Let's hope it was informative and able to provide you with all of the tools you need to achieve your goals of learning to analyze people.

The next step is to take what you have learned and begin to see people around you for what they really are. It will also help you know if people are lying and trying to deceive you.

Finally, if you found this book useful in any way, a review on Amazon is always appreciated!